Searchlight
BOOKS

Exploring Robotics

Robots at Home

Liz Sonneborn

Lerner Publications ◆ Minneapolis

To Rosemary

Lerner Publications Company
An imprint of Lerner Publishing Group, Inc.
241 First Avenue North
Minneapolis, MN 55401 USA

For reading levels and more information, look up this title at www.lernerbooks.com.

Main body text set in Adrianna Regular.
Typeface provided by Chank.

Library of Congress Cataloging-in-Publication Data

Names: Sonneborn, Liz, author.
Title: Robots at home / Liz Sonneborn.
Description: Minneapolis : Lerner Publications , [2024] | Series: Searchlight books - exploring robotics | Includes bibliographical references and index. | Audience: Ages 8–11 | Audience: Grades 4–6 | Summary: "Domestic robots come in many varieties, from robots that clean homes to fun robot dogs! Readers learn all about them and how they can clean, take care of people, and even be pets"— Provided by publisher.
Identifiers: LCCN 2022042814 (print) | LCCN 2022042815 (ebook) | ISBN 9781728476797 (lib. bdg.) | ISBN 9798765603673 (pbk.) | ISBN 9798765600115 (eb pdf)
Subjects: LCSH: Robots—Juvenile literature.
Classification: LCC TJ211.2 .S663 2024 (print) | LCC TJ211.2 (ebook) | DDC 629.8/92—dc23/eng/20220930

LC record available at https://lccn.loc.gov/2022042814
LC ebook record available at https://lccn.loc.gov/2022042815

Manufactured in the United States of America
1-52260-50700-11/2/2022

Table of Contents

Chapter 1

HARD AT WORK

The house is clean. The laundry is done. Dinner is on the table. And no one lifted a finger to make it happen.

That might be hard to imagine. But someday robots might take over these chores. These machines are built to perform specific tasks. Robots that work in the home are called domestic robots.

Getting the Job Done

For many years, scientists have been designing and building domestic robots. In the 1980s, hobbyists built HERO robots from a kit. One model, the Hero Jr., could sing songs, recite nursery rhymes, and wake a person up at a certain time. In the late 1990s, children were introduced to Furby, a fuzzy robotic toy with its own language.

Furby robots came in many colors.

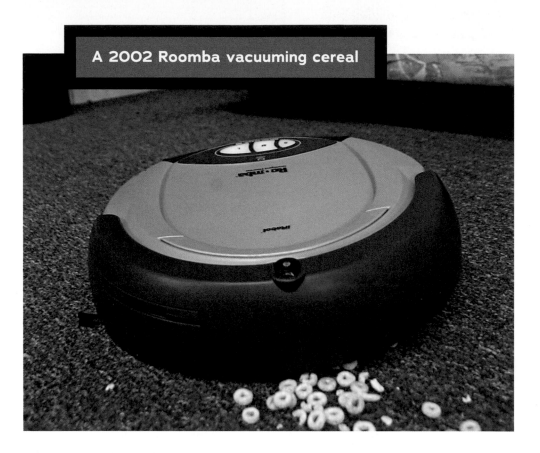

A 2002 Roomba vacuuming cereal

The first popular cleaning robot was Roomba. Beginning in 2002, people could buy a Roomba to vacuum their floors. Sometimes early robot vacuums would actually spread messes around rather than cleaning them up. But the latest versions are better at detecting messes and cleaning them or avoiding them if it's something they can't vacuum.

Like robot vacuums, most cleaning robots perform just one task. But these tasks are often messy, long, or dangerous. Robot helpers can get them done quickly and safely.

STEM Spotlight

The first robot vacuums zigzagged across the floor, often missing spots. Newer models, such as the Roomba 980, work better. Its camera takes pictures as its moves. Its computer uses these images to make a map of the room. The map lets the robot know where it is, so it does not vacuum the same area twice. When its battery runs low, the map also helps the vacuum find its charger.

Robot lawn mowers cut grass. Robot snowplows clear driveways and sidewalks. Robots can also clean windows, storm gutters, and barbeque grills. Some cat owners are happy to have self-cleaning robot litter boxes relieve them of the smelly chore.

A robot litter box will clean itself after a cat uses it.

A person making a video call on Astro

Smart Robots

Some newer robots can perform more than one task. Astro went on sale in 2021. About 2 feet (0.6 m) tall, it looks like a computer tablet on wheels. Astro can place video calls, set alarms, play music, and even perform a little dance. It is also a home security robot. People can use the camera on its arm to monitor their home when they are away.

Astro has artificial intelligence (AI). This allows it to respond to speech and decide how to move through a room. Astro can also recognize human faces.

Robots may one day be able to clean a whole house.

Because of AI, domestic robots are getting smarter. But they still have trouble doing things that are easy for many people. For example, most robots cannot climb stairs or reliably grip objects. This limits what even the smartest domestic robots can do.

Chapter 2

TEACHERS AND CAREGIVERS

Domestic robots do more than clean a home. They can also help humans by teaching them new skills or attending to their needs.

Learning from Robots

Adults often feel awkward talking to a robot. But many children are comfortable with it. This makes children good students for robot teachers.

Charlie is a social robot. People can talk to robots like Charlie and Moxie.

One of these is Moxie. It has a squat body and a large head. Its cartoonlike face appears on a screen. Moxie's face can mimic human emotions. Its mouth can form a smile. It can raise its eyebrows to show surprise.

Moxie tells stories, shares fun facts, and cracks jokes. It can help children who have trouble communicating. By talking to Moxie, they can learn how to talk with other people.

STEM Spotlight

The little Cozmo robot is a fun playmate. It can sing and play games. But it also can introduce children to a valuable skill—computer coding. Code is a set of instructions a person gives to a computer. Through coding, people make computers complete tasks. Cozmo's Code Lab provides simple coding to control the robot. With the right code, Cozmo can be made to sneeze, do math problems, and recognize colors.

Dash is another robot teacher. It helps kids build problem-solving skills through games and puzzles. ClicBot is a robot that teaches about robots! It has thirty-five types of parts that users can put together in different ways to make all sorts of robot toys.

Users can practice coding with Dash through apps.

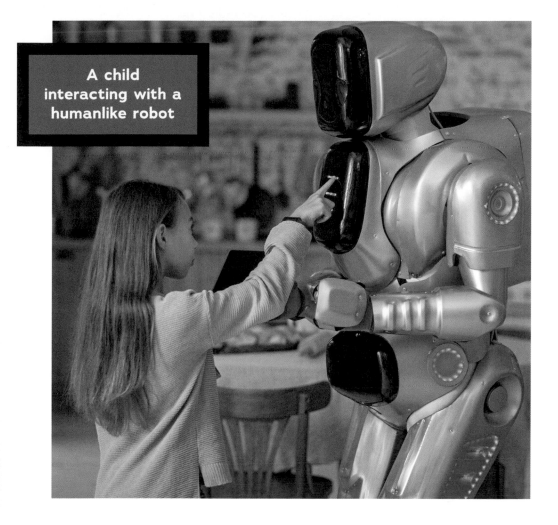

A child interacting with a humanlike robot

Robot Helpers

Some domestic robots help with childcare. For example, the 5e NannyBot helps people watch their kids. The robot follows children as they move through their home. Its camera sends video and audio clips that let an adult in another room see what the children are up to and talk to them.

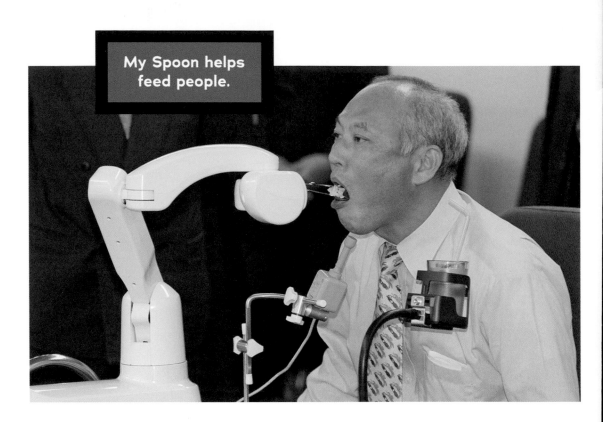

My Spoon helps feed people.

Robots can also assist people with disabilities. My Spoon helps people who cannot use their hands. Its robot arm scoops up food and carries it to a person's mouth. People can operate the arm by moving a joystick with other limbs or their chin.

Other robots assist many people such as older adults, those living alone, people with disabilities, and more. Pria dispenses medicine. Its voice reminds people to take their pills. Budgee carries groceries and other items. It can follow someone who uses a wheelchair through a store or a home.

Chapter 3

MAKING FRIENDS WITH ROBOTS

Domestic robots are more than just workers and helpers. Sometimes humans consider them fun companions or even friends.

Pet-Like Pals

Some domestic robots look and act like pets. One of the most popular is Aibo. This robot puppy performs tricks and recognizes humans. Over time, it gains its own personality just like a real dog.

Paro is another pet-like robot. This furry gadget looks like a baby harp seal. When it sits in a person's lap, it wriggles, coos, and bats its long eyelashes.

Paro may look like a toy. But it is often used as a medical device. It helps calm people suffering from depression and other medical conditions. Petting a Paro can also soothe stress in older people with memory loss and children with disabilities.

Many people like to pet Paro.

Key Figure

Toshitada Doi is a Japanese engineer best known as the creator of Aibo, the famed robotic dog toy. Born in 1943, he began working for Sony Japan in 1964. He helped invent the compact disc (CD). In the 1990s, he was the head of Sony's Digital Creatures Laboratory. His team made robot versions of living things such as dogs. After his success with Aibo, Doi invented Qrio in 2003. This humanoid robot once acted in *Astro Boy* on Japanese television.

People talking to Pepper, a social robot

Robot Companions

Some domestic robots keep people company who live by themselves or spend a lot of time alone. These social robots can make people feel less lonely by talking to them and providing emotional support.

The ElliQ is a social robot created for older people. It looks like a small lamp with a computer tablet. ElliQ performs tasks such as placing video calls or displaying information or pictures on its screen.

ElliQ makes conversation. It tells jokes and plays games. It also gently encourages healthful habits. It might remind a person to drink water, take medicine, and get more sleep. ElliQ even remembers a person's favorite things and brings them up in conversation, just as a friend might.

An ElliQ robot

A child touches a model robot's hand at a 2022 show.

Getting Too Close?

Some people might prefer a robot to a human companion. Friends and family can get impatient and annoyed. Robot companions are always calm and upbeat.

But robot companions have some downsides. Robots do not have or experience feelings. Even though robots can make people feel less lonely, they cannot replace real contact with other humans.

Chapter 4

WHAT'S NEXT

In 2019, Jibo, a small social robot, made a video. It said goodbye to its fans. The company that made Jibo did not make enough money to keep selling the robot. Jibo's fate is common. Few domestic robots have caught on with the public.

Questioning Domestic Robots

Domestic robots cost hundreds or even thousands of dollars. For most families, they are too expensive for the limited tasks they can perform.

Some people also have privacy concerns. Domestic robots often record images of a home's layout. This allows them to move without running into walls and furniture. But some homeowners fear an intruder could hack the robot's computer system and get this information.

A Jibo robot. Like many domestic robots, Jibo wasn't popular enough to keep producing.

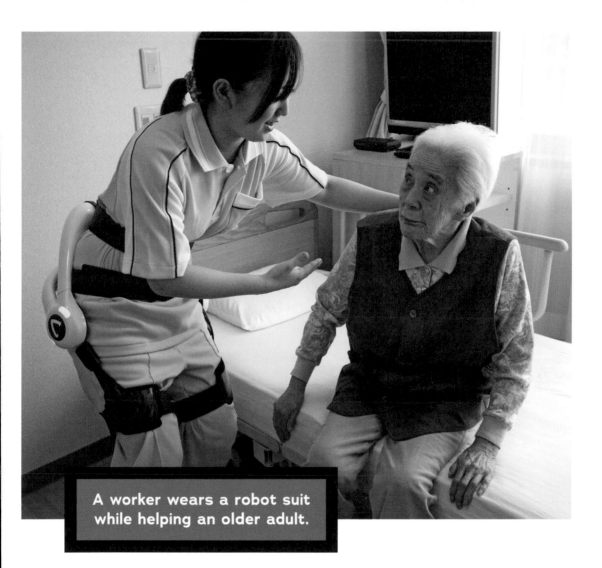

A worker wears a robot suit while helping an older adult.

Many people are not comfortable sharing their homes with a robot. A 2018 survey found that 68 percent of American participants did not want a robot that could perform household chores. Eighty-four percent did not want robots providing care for a family member or loved one.

Newer and Better

Despite some concerns, people will likely become more comfortable with domestic robots in the future. The population of older adults is growing. There will not be enough human workers to help with older people's

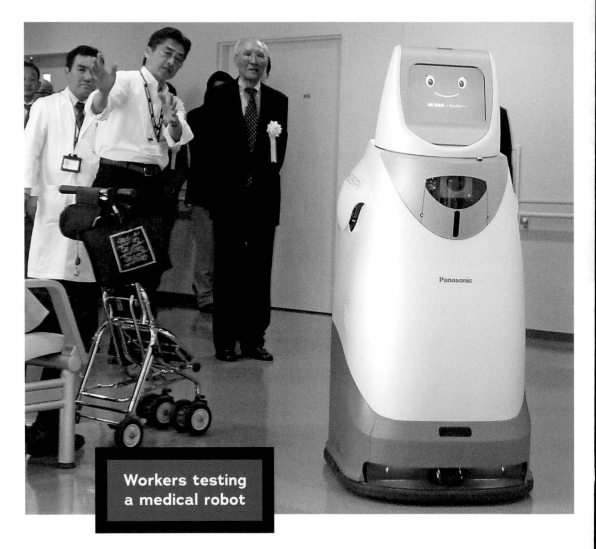

Workers testing a medical robot

People might one day need more help from robots at home.

health care and other daily needs. People may have to turn to robots for help.

Many companies are creating new robots for this care. One called Stretch will be able to dress a person. Other tasks robots could help with include feeding meals, bathing, and taking people to the bathroom.

A modern robot vacuum

Domestic robots are improving. Newer robots will likely be able to learn how to do many chores instead of just one or two. By watching a human make a bed or set a table, they might one day be able to pick up these skills on their own.

As robots become better and cheaper, more people will likely purchase them for their homes. Robotics scientists and engineers are excited about the future.

A father and son have fun playing with a toy robot.

Glossary

artificial intelligence: the ability of a robot or computer to learn and make decisions

companion: someone with whom a person spends a lot of time

conversation: a talk between two or more people

disability: a condition that limits a person's ability to do certain things

domestic: having to do with the home

hack: to use a computer to gain access to information without permission

hobbyist: someone who engages in an interest or activity such as building robots for pleasure

privacy: freedom from being seen or disturbed

robot: machines that can perform specific tasks independently or with limited instruction from humans

social: suited to seeking relationships with others

Learn More

Awesome 8 Rad Robots
   https://kids.nationalgeographic.com/awesome-8/article/robots

Britannica Kids: Robot
   https://kids.britannica.com/kids/article/robot/353723

Hamilton, S. L. *Household Robots*. Minneapolis: Abdo, 2019.

Idzikowski, Lisa. *Competition Robots*. Minneapolis: Lerner Publications, 2024.

Martin, Emmett. *Robots All around Us: From Medicine to the Military*. Buffalo: Gareth Stevens, 2023.

Robotics: Facts
   https://sciencetrek.org/sciencetrek/topics/robots/facts.cfm

Index

Photo Acknowledgments

Image credits: PA Images/Alamy Stock Photo, p. 5; Douglas McFadd/Getty Images, p. 6; Thorsten Nilson/EyeEm/Getty Images, p. 8; Amazon, p. 9; Maciej Frolow/Getty Images, p. 10; PHILIP FONG/AFP/Getty Images, p. 12; Friso Gentsch/picture alliance/Getty Images, p. 14; Dmytro Zinkevych/Alamy Stock Photo, p. 15; STR/AFP/Getty Images, p. 16; KAZUHIRO NOGI/AFP/Getty Images, p. 18; The Asahi Shimbun/Getty Images, p. 19; Laura De Meo/Alamy Stock Photo, p. 20; MANDEL NGAN/AFP/Getty Images, p. 21; Lyu Ming/China News Service/Getty Images, p. 22; Joan Cros/NurPhoto/Getty Images, p. 24; YOSHIKAZU TSUNO/AFP/Getty Images, p. 25; Kyodo News Stills/Getty Images, p. 26; miriam-doerr/Getty Images, p. 27; RuslanDashinsky/Getty Images, p. 28; Westend61/Getty Images, p. 29.

Cover: Boyer/Roger Viollet/Getty Images.